George Miller

A Sermon Preached Before His Excellency Charles, Marquis Cornwallis

Lord Lieutenant, President and the Members of the Association for...

George Miller

A Sermon Preached Before His Excellency Charles, Marquis Cornwallis
Lord Lieutenant, President and the Members of the Association for...

ISBN/EAN: 9783337002619

Printed in Europe, USA, Canada, Australia, Japan

Cover: Foto ©Lupo / pixelio.de

More available books at **www.hansebooks.com**

A

SERMON

PREACHED BEFORE

HIS EXCELLENCY

CHARLES, MARQUIS CORNWALLIS,

LORD LIEUTENANT, *PRESIDENT*,

AND THE

MEMBERS

OF THE

ASSOCIATION

FOR

DISCOUNTENANCING VICE, AND PROMOTING THE
PRACTICE OF RELIGION AND VIRTUE;

IN

St. WERBURGH's CHURCH,

ON THURSDAY 23d MAY, 1799.

BY THE

REV. GEORGE MILLER, D.D. F.T.C.

————≫≫≫≫≫≋≪≪≪≪≪————

DUBLIN:

PRINTED FOR WILLIAM WATSON AND SON,

PRINTERS TO THE ASSOCIATION,

NO. 7, CAPEL-STREET.

———

1799.

At an Extraordinary Meeting of *the Affociation for difcountenancing Vice and promoting the Practice of Religion and Virtue*, held in St. Werburgh's Veftry-Room, 23d May, 1799.

His Grace the Lord Primate, in the Chair.

It was Unanimoufly Refolved,

On the motion of His Grace the Lord Archbifhop of Tuam, feconded by the Right Rev. and Hon. the Lord Bifhop of Cork,

That the Thanks of this Affociation be prefented to the Rev. GEORGE MILLER, D. D. F. T. C. for his excellent Sermon preached before them this Day, and that he be requefted to publifh the fame.

Signed by Order,

JAMES MAXWELL,
WILLIAM MATURIN, } Secretaries.

SERMON, &c.

PSALM iv. 6.

" There be many that say, who will shew us any
" good? Lord, lift thou up the light of thy
" countenance upon us."

IN this eventful time *there are* indeed *many
that say, who will shew us any good?* This is
not merely the desponding inquiry of individuals, suffering the casualties and distresses of
private life. The great masses of mankind,
whose prosperity and adversity seem to be regulated by surer laws, are now prompted by
the wide-extended feeling of political calamity, to look around with anxiety for some
wise monitor, who would teach them *the things
which belong unto their peace.* Throughout the
whole extent of the civilized world, through-

B   out

out all thofe regions in which the improve-
ments of arts and policy correfpond to the
dignity of a reafonable nature, one melancholy fcene of actual hoftility or of apprehenfion, of internal convulfion or of foreign violence, prefents itfelf to the reflecting mind.
Even the nations which flumbered in the tor-
por of barbarifm, have been forced into this
tremendous conteft of human paffion. The
difturbers of Europe have penetrated the de-
farts of the eaftern world, and have carried
among the debafements of almoft favage manners the madnefs of corrupted civilization.

In fuch an awful period of human affairs,
*when the hearts of men are failing them for fear,
and for looking after the things which are coming
upon the earth*, they muft be blind indeed, who
will place their entire confidence in the efficacy
of thofe fecondary caufes, which, in ordinary
and peaceful times, appear fufficient for the
maintenance of public tranquillity. When
the world is changing around us, when among
other nations all the temporal refources of political fafety have failed in fucceffion, and
events unufual and portentous crowd fo faft
upon our notice, that we are furprized if,

during

during any little interval, no fubverted government lengthens the difaftrous roll of revolution, great muft be the blindnefs and prefumption of thofe, who will ftill rely for their fecurity on the petty expedients of human wifdom. The vifitations of the Almighty have accordingly turned unto him the thoughts of the ferious and reflecting. The conviction of the temporal, if not of the eternal, importance of chriftianity, has been impreffed upon the minds even of thofe who heretofore had lived in a thoughtlefs difregard of its momentous communications. Perfons of every rank have been taught to entertain the fentiment of the Pfalmift; and that *the Lord would lift up the light of his countenance upon us*, that his favour fhould be conciliated by a more ftrict conformity to his facred will, is beginning to be regarded as the fureft pledge of political fecurity.

The Affociation, which I am appointed to addrefs this day, were early convinced of the urgent and indifpenfable neceffity of an effort to reanimate the decaying principle of religious obligation. More than fix years ago a very fmall number of individuals lamented

the

the rapid and alarming progrefs of immorality and impiety, and fought in the united endeavours of thofe who fhould be actuated by a kindred feeling, that ability to ftem the torrent, which they were fenfible their detached exertions never could poffefs. The virtuous call has been favourably received, and eagerly obeyed. It muft naturally be expected, that the clerical order fhould be forward in connecting themfelves with an Affociation, whofe object is to accomplifh more effectually the very purpofe, to which their own labours had been confecrated. They muft have been falfe to the truft which has been repofed in them by the community, they muft have been unprofitable fervants of that God whofe worfhip they profefs to inculcate, if they had not zealoufly combined their powers with thofe of an Affociation " for difcountenancing vice and promoting the practice of religion and virtue." But happily our Inftitution is not compofed only of perfons of this defcription. The facred importance of its object has interefted in its caufe the talents and refpectability of the various departments of focial life, and three fucceffive Vice-roys have deemed the protection and encouragement of its exertions worthy

thy of the reprefentative of Majefty. It is my duty to ftate to an Affociation thus diftin-guifhed by all that can beftow dignity on a fociety, dignified by the noblenefs of its purpofes and by the rank of its patrons, what are thofe confiderations which render the utmoft energy of their exertions effentially important, and in what manner the exertions of fuch an Affociation may be effectual to the attainment of the ends which they propofe. It is a fub-ject which has been ably treated by my prede-ceffors, but the repeated difcuffion of it may not be unufeful. To the members of the Affociation it may perhaps contribute to re-new that vigorous zeal, which is liable to abatement in every long-continued effort; and with the public in general it may ferve to diffufe more widely an intereft in the objects of this Affociation, and thus at once to extend that moral influence which fuch an intereft muft create in the minds in which it has been excited, and by the more powerful co-opera-tion of ftill larger numbers, to render more efficient thofe means by which the Inftitution labours to invigorate the feeling of religious obligation.

Look

Look abroad then into the world, my brethren, and reflect on its situation. Wherever you turn your eyes, you behold thofe focial combinations, in which alone man can attain to the dignity of his nature, in which he finds the opportunity of his exertion and the means of his improvement, menacing their fpeedy diffolution into the elemental war of anarchy and rudenefs. At home we behold the melancholy veftiges of a fanguinary rebellion, which, whilft it defied the reftraints of government, outraged every feeling of humanity and virtue. Who that confiders thefe things will not acknowledge that fome principle is wanting, which fhall chain down the violence of human paffion, and bind more clofely to each other the members of each community ?

If reafon did not inform us that the ftrong principle, which can alone fecure to a nation the bleffings of internal tranquillity, is an extended regard to religious obligation, practical experience would fupply with the fimple evidence of fact abundant means of conviction. What nation is that, whofe convulfive ftruggles have fpread through the world diforder

and

and difmay, which feems by its fufferings to be the providential warning, and by its violences to be the providential chaftifement of the prefent age? The fame in which it is notorious that the moft avowed difregard of revealed religion had long prevailed; in which to defpife and ridicule the gofpel of Chrift had been confidered as an indifpenfable accomplifhment of polifhed life, and profligacy of manners had been fanctioned by ufage, and methodifed into fyftem: the fame which has exhibited to the world the moral prodigy of an European government formally difcarding, as an exploded artifice, the fublime fimplicity of the chriftian revelation, and fubftituting in the place of its folemnities the childifh pageantries of heathen idolatry: the fame which, to promote the fchemes of its ambition, has affected to range itfelf under the banners of the impoftor of the Eaft; and, though too much enlightened for the gofpel of Chrift, could accommodate its pliant acquiefcence to that mafs of voluptuoufnefs, extravagance and plagiarifm, the koran of Mahomet. I fay not this for the purpofe of exciting or cherifhing any violent fpirit of national antipathy even againft thofe enemies of our peace: but,

whilft

whilſt in the mildneſs of chriſtian charity we
deplore their infatuated perverſeneſs, we may
derive from their example the inſtructive ad-
monition, that the diſregard of divine revelation is fatal to the peace, and good order, and
happineſs of human ſociety.

This impreſſive leſſon of immediate obſer-
vation is corroborated by every conſideration
of the nature of human ſociety. In vain may
the abſtracted philoſopher argue to his own
theoretical conviction, that every man will
moſt effectually promote his private enjoyment,
by withdrawing his view from his own individual intereſts, and labouring with his utmoſt
energy for the advancement of the general
good. The rapacity of the violent, the in-
trigue of the artful, and even the innocent
ſuffering of the poor, will proteſt againſt the
ſpeculative concluſion. Will the man of violence liſten with unimpaſſioned fairneſs to the
argument which would perſuade him to ſub-
mit to the labours of induſtry, and await its
ſlow advantages? Will the corrupt man be
induced to forego the ſuperiority, which he
derives from diſhoneſty and cunning, and
content himſelf with his proportioned ſhare of

the

the general profperity? Will the victim of poverty and diftrefs feel that a patient acquiefcence under the heavy preffure of affliction, as it unqueftionably would conduce to the public order and happinefs of fociety, would alfo be the moft effectual method of affuaging his forrows and fatisfying his wants? The various propenfities, which urge men to the feparation of private from public good, may indeed be reftrained ; but not by any reflections on its theoretical impracticability. The fear of the great judge of all the earth may arreft the arm of the ruffian, check the fcheme of the fraudulent, and reprefs the impatience of the deftitute. Inftead of an intricate and doubtful connection of their private welfare with the profperity of a community, they may perceive a fure and inevitable connection between their good or evil conduct, and the retributions of an all-feeing God—The influence of human laws muft be ineffectual, if it be not directed and enforced by the paramount authority of the divine commands. Without the pervading influence of religious obligation, human law is but the interefted combination of the powerful to compel the obedience of the multitude. If the legiflator

be

be not actuated by religious confiderations, the law itself may be oppreffive; and if the people be irreligious, the great fecurity of evidence is loft, nor will the law be executed with fidelity. It is not the fubftitute, but the fupplement, of the divine law. It pre-fuppofes the general prevalence of religious obligation, and merely directs its operation to the various exigencies of the public.

It is effential therefore to the well-being of fociety, that its members fhould be bound together by a principle more authoritative than the fpeculations of philofophy, more perfect and coercive than the mere regulations of legiflation. Whatever may be the contentions of human politics, the men who fincerely and zealoufly labour to revive this principle where it has decayed, are true patriots. They labour to eftablifh in the hearts of men that unerring rule of conduct, which fo far as its influence extends muft be eminently beneficial, and without which the wifeft efforts of the worldly politician muft be fruitlefs. Let me then direct your attention to the manner in which our Affociation is fitted to operate upon the public mind; let me point out to you its powerful

erful tendency to the gradual correction of thofe oppofite extremes of thoughtlefs irreligion and fuperftitious bigotry, which difgrace the different claffes of our countrymen.

That the indulgences of affluence, and the vanities of fuperior ftation, are unfavourable to the call of chiftian piety, is a maxim which requires from the preacher no tedious difcuffion. In the hour of ferious meditation all muft admit its truth, whilft all are yet eager to expofe themfelves in the dangerous fituation. Surrounded by the affiduous attentions of dependants, the elevated are ill-fitted for receiving impreffions of chriftian humility. Commanding every indulgence of appetite or caprice, the affluent are unfuited to that regulated fobriety of temper, which regards this life but as a pilgrimage to the true refting-place of a reafonable creature. The prefent world puts forth for the exalted all its charms, and the utmoft energy of a moral and religious mind is requifite for difpelling the fafcinating magic of the fcene, and preffing forward to man's real deftination. Unhappily the influence of thefe feductions is not confined to thofe who are immediately expofed to their operation.

operation. Not only the few who are placed
in the more elevated ftations of fociety, are in
danger of forgetting, amidft the diffipations
of pleafure and the delufions of adulation,
that ferious and folemn duty of *working out
their falvation* with earneft folicitude, to which
all of every rank are equally exhorted. The
ftrong contagion of example diffufes through
many inferior orders the effects of thofe temptations, which act with their principal force
only on the moft exalted ; and the habitual irreligion of unthinking and worldly-minded
luxury defcends from rank to rank, until it
penetrates to the very centre of the focial
fyftem.

Such being the difpofitions which the circumftances of the higher orders are too well
fitted to infpire, fome other rule of conduct muft be introduced, which fhall be
lefs rigorous in its impofitions of forbearance,
and lefs mortifying to the pride of ftation,
than the felf-denying doctrine of a crucified
Redeemer; fome compromife between the en-
joyments of this life and the hopes of futurity ;
fome fyftem which may accommodate itfelf to
every propenfity, and afford a juftification to
every

every indulgence. Such is the law of honour, the all-fwaying rule of worldly opinion, which is worfhipped with idolatrous veneration. Originating perhaps at a remote period in the purity of chriftian morals operating on the rudenefs of a barbarous world, it is at this day the mere regifter of the prevailing practices of the fafhionable orders. Conftituted by their own conduct, it can enjoin no fevere reftriction on the indulgence of appetite. It can authorize the exceffes of the drunkard, the pillage of the gamefter, the irreligion of the man of the world, the corruption of the felfifh man, the licentioufnefs of the man of gallantry, and the murder of the duellift. It is a law derived from thofe actions which it ought to regulate, and enforced by the appro-bation of thofe whom it ought to reftrain.

Such a rule of vicious indulgence and mu-tual countenance, fuch a confpiracy againft the genuine principles of moral and religious duty, meets in this Affociation, if it be zea-loufly fupported, its proper and adequate counteraction. That opinion which gives its fanction to vice and irreligion, is here oppof-ed by a declaration of opinion in favour of religion

religion and morality. The licentious are no longer permitted to prescribe laws to the serious and devout. The friends of religion are here associated in opposition to the sneer of the dissipated, and avow to the world their determination *to hearken unto God rather than unto man.* ▪If all that respectability of rank and talent, which graces the rolls of our Institution, be faithfully employed for the attainment of its objects, soon will the law of opinion become the ally, instead of the enemy of religion; soon will the voice of fashion afford its aid to the cause of virtue, and the higher classes of the community be honourably distinguished by a concern for the true interests and happiness of man.

Among the laborious poor the obstructions, which impede the influence of religion, are of a very different kind, but not less within the power of our Association. Ignorance is the grand enemy of the religion of the poor. Whilst every exertion is engrossed by the necessity of providing the daily means of subsistence, their thoughts are confined to the urgent concerns of the passing day, unless some messenger of good or ill should labour

to

to inculcate principles of virtue or of vice. The poor are indeed placed in a fituation not unfavourable to the impreffions of religion. Little attached to a world which for them poffeffes little charms, they can eafily be induced to embrace that covenant of mercy, which proffers to them another life of everlaft- ing happinefs. The pleafures of the prefent fcene do not bribe them from its acceptance, nor does the pride of prefumptuous reafon teach them to cavil at its terms. But it fhould be remembered that the fituation of the poor man is at leaft equally favourable to the leffons of turbulence and outrage. Whilft fuffering the fatigues of labour and the hardfhips of poverty, he is tempted to compare his circum- ftances with the eafe and accommodations of the opulent. Ignorance may ftupify his reafon, but will not moderate his paffions. That ine- quality of human conditions, which philofo- phy might fhew to be unavoidable, and in which religion might teach him to acquiefce with patient refignation, he is eafily indu- ced to regard as a fyftem of injuftice and op- preffion. He cannot with the fpeculative poli- tician review the hiftory of human fociety, and difcover that irreverfible decree which has

diftributed

diftributed its members into claffes diftin-
guifhed from each other with fuch apparent
partiality of favour. He is unable to perceive
the fallacy of thofe fchemes, by which the
agents of public diforder tell him that his fituation may be improved. Unufed to the complicated confideration of political caufes and
effects, he fees only what to him appears one
great and intolerable grievance, and which
he doubts not that one great effort will effectually remove—Unhappily for our country,
this is no imaginary picture, it is not now the
mere apprehenfion of a fpeculator anxious to
juftify by the poffibility of public mifchief
fome favourite fcheme of public improvement.
It is now matter of record, and is regiftered in
the annals of the nation. Perufe that moft interefting detail of the confpiracy, which was
laft year fo providentially blafted when almoft ripe for execution, and you will learn
that the poor of this ifland had been feduced
into a participation of its plans by no confideration of the general advantages of political in-
novation, but fimply by a perfuafion artfully
inculcated, that their own particular fituation
fhould be meliorated in the general convulfion,
that in the promifcuous confufion of all orders
and

and diftinctions *the poor fhould ceafe out of the land*, that the pillage of the affluent fhould fupply them with the enjoyment of the neceffaries and comforts of life, and that after this one great violation of the rights of property every man fhould thenceforward continue in the undifturbed poffeffion of his portion of the plunder.

What effectual remedy can be propofed for an evil, which thus undermines the very foundation of civilized fociety, which rouzes, by delufive promifes of unattainable advantages, the phyfical force of the multitude againft the fecurity of property and the authority of law? —If it were juftifiable to adopt a deliberate fcheme of human degradation, if it were allowable to decree that man, whom the Almighty had formed *in his own image*, reafonable and immortal, fhould for the peace and good order of fociety be reduced to the rank of a machine; it muft now be impracticable. You cannot do it. You cannot fhut the ear to the fecret inftigations of fedition. You cannot raze from the memory the recollection of thofe maxims of public confufion, which laft year defolated a wide portion of your country

C   —Were

—Were no fuch confiderations applicable to our fituation, I fhould not be an advocate for the unnatural fyftem, which would fecure the good conduct by fhackling the under-ftandings of the poor. Shall the great majo-rity of our fpecies be debafed and embruted, as the only method by which they can be qua-lified for their ftation in fociety ? Is the light of reafon given to them only to be extin-guifhed ? Are they incapable of apprehending thofe fimple, yet fublime, leffons of piety to-wards God and charity towards man, which the fcriptures of our religion have recorded for our edification ? Are their intervals from labour to be abandoned to the ftupidity of floth, or to the riot of in-toxication ; and is no opportunity to be afford-ed to them of foothing by the comforting af-furances of the gofpel the difcontents of po-verty and fatigue ?—But this is a fyftem, which now has few fupporters. The enemies of peace and order have left us no alternative but that of a wide-extended diffufion of moral and religious inftruction. The fpirit of delu-fion is gone forth, and the true fpirit, that of chriftian piety, can alone defeat its efforts. For this purpofe the fcriptures muft be made as much as poffible the companions of your people.

The

The poor muſt be enabled to become familiar with thoſe intereſting narratives which ſo beautifully diſplay the mild and amiable affections of the human heart, with thoſe awful inſtances of divine retribution which manifeſt a providential ſuperintendance of the moſt ſecret actions of mankind, with thoſe affecting effuſions of fervent and humble piety which ſo powerfully excite the ſympathies of every ſerious and unvitiated mind, and with thoſe ineſtimable aſſurances of ſalvation which can alleviate every hardſhip, and miniſter conſolation in every ſuffering. You cannot meet the political incendiary on merely equal terms. You cannot by political diſcuſſion expoſe to the conviction of the peaſant the miſchievous futility of the ſcheme, by which he is ſtimulated to the work of blood. He feels that poverty and labour are diſtreſſing, but cannot comprehend the complicated theory of human ſociety which requires that the many ſhould labour for the few. The partiſan of outrage appeals only to his ſenſes and his paſſions. The friend of peace and order muſt fail, if he ſhould oppoſe to theſe ſtrong impulſes nothing but an appeal to an underſtanding unuſed to abſtracted reaſoning and incapable of compre-

hending

hending its force. But what cannot be effected
with the underftanding, may be accomplifhed
with the heart. Religion will point out to the
poor man the Saviour of the world wandering
without having where to lay his head, and he will
feel his own fufferings dignified and alleviated
by the great example. Religion will teach him
to regard whatever feverities may attend his
lot as the trials of a kind though correcting
providence, and to reft affured that his patient
endurance fhould hereafter receive ample retribution. The genuine language of religion
will harmonize every feeling, and bid the
ftormy war of paffion ceafe. Inftead of fpecu-
lating on political confequences, the poor will
be habituated to meditate on religious duties.
That their fituation is the will of God, and
that refignation and induftry are their duties,
are principles which will enable them to repel
the pernicious infinuations, which would be-
tray them into the miferies and crimes of civil
war. The fpirit of religion fhall move over
the troubled face of our country, and order
and light fhall emerge from the moral chaos.

This fole effectual remedy of the turbulence
of the lower claffes was among the earlieft objects

jects of our Affociation. Its utmoft efforts
have been exerted to encourage the catechetical
inftruction of children in the principles of the
chriftian religion, and by the well regulated
diftribution of prizes much has been effected
in the metropolis and its vicinity. But the
evil required a more comprehenfive plan of
reformation. This, though highly important,
was confined in a great meafure to the adopted children of public charity, to thofe who
had been placed in the different inftitutions for
the protection of the indigent. To reach the
mafs of the people, to produce that general effect which could alone counteract the general
diforder, the Affociation adopted the meafures
moft conducive to fuccefs. Short tracts on
moral and religious fubjects have in confiderable
numbers been fpread throughout the country,
and a very extended diftribution of the holy
fcriptures themfelves has been undertaken and
accomplifhed. With chriftian earneftnefs you
addreffed the public for their fupport. You
difclaimed the propagation of the tenets of
any particular fect. You profeffed a nobler
purpofe " than making profelytes from any
one perfuafion of chriftians to another."
Your plan was, " to diffeminate more exten-
fively,

fively, than had ever yet been done, " THE
WORD OF GOD, and to make effectual provifi-
on, that no houfe, no cabin in the whole
kingdom, in which there is a fingle perfon
who can read, fhould be deftitute of the holy
fcriptures."

Thus is our Affociation a moral inftrument
well adapted to the melioration of every clafs
of the community. Comprifing among its
members perfons diftinguifhed by all the refpectability of ftation and of talent, it is fitted
to fhame from fociety that extravagant and
impious notion, which, in avowed difregard of
the revelations of the Almighty, would erect
into a formal ftandard of human conduct the
actual practices of the diffipated and licentious.
Embodying into one united effort the zealous
endeavours of every individual folicitous for
the profperity of his country, and for the
everlafting falvation of the ignorant and deluded, it is fitted to exert a powerful and well
directed influence upon every part of the great
fyftem of the public. It is fitted, if its plan
be duly fupported by the fincerity and zeal of
its members, to abafh the effrontery of fafhionable

onable vice, and to eradicate the crimes of deluded ignorance.

But there are some peculiar circumstances in the state of society in this country, which render the operation of such an Association in a superior degree important to the diffusion of religious principle.

One of the characteristic circumstances, which distinguish the general state of society in this country, is that it is composed in a considerable degree of those extreme orders, which form the basis and the pinnacle of improved and polished life ; that it is a combination of the habits and manners of the more elevated and of the humbler ranks, with little of that regular gradation of intermediate classes, which might by imperceptible transitions connect the two extremes. The influence of this circumstance upon the political situation of our country has been frequently the subject of consideration. Its operation upon the state of religion has been less attentively examined. Let me then direct your thoughts to this view of society in Ireland, and point out to you the peculiar utility of our Associa-

tion

ion in remedying the moral mifchief, which may appear to refult from the comparative deficiency of the middle orders of focial life.

It is an old remark, that the middle rank is moft favourable to the influence of virtue. *Give me,* faid Agur, *neither poverty nor riches, feed me with food convenient for me ; left I be full, and deny thee, and fay, Who is the Lord ? or left I be poor, and fteal, and take the name of my God in vain.* Affailed on either fide by the enemies of its influence over the hearts of men, coun-teracted on the one part by the temptations of diftrefs, and on the other by the pomps and in-dulgences of an alluring world, the genuine fpirit of religion has in general its moft exten-five and operative fway over the middle claffes of the community, over thofe who are raifed above the neceffities of the loweft, and depreffed beneath the luxuries of the higheft fituations. In the moft elevated ranks many individuals do indeed approve themfelves diftinguifhed inftances of real piety and active charity, but a fair confideration of human infirmity will not fuffer us to expect that thefe difpofitions fhould be generally prevalent in circumftances fo unfavourable to their operation. The higher orders

orders may be indifpenfable for perfecting the political machine, by beftowing upon the community the refinements of improved fociety, by animating with the encouraging hope of diftinction the exertions of induftry and genius, and by maintaining that equilibrium of oppofing interefts which conduces to the tranquillity of a ftate ; but the faving influence of chriftian piety will ever emanate moft powerfully from the moderation of the middle claffes. As their fober induftry and regulated frugality are the very ftamina of the political profperity of a nation, fo is their ferious and confcientious regard to chriftian duty the fureft bafis of national religion.

What then muft be the ftate of religion in a country in which thefe claffes are comparatively lefs numerous ? Is it not in fuch a community expofed to peculiar dangers ? Does it not require for its fupport extraordinary exertions from thofe who are indeed zealous in its caufe ? Is it not neceffary that its friends fhould by their activity and co-operation endeavour to compenfate the deficiency ; to diffufe around them with more ftrenuous exertions that religious influence, which local, as well as general
ral

ral caufes, fo powerfully tend to counteract and to deftroy? Such a fyftem of religious activity and co-operation is our Affociation. Here every man who is zealous for the advancement of religion, who is indeed fincere in his profeffion of the chriftian faith, who believes that the everlafting happinefs of mankind is concerned in its reception, and that even their temporal profperity is beft promoted by a ftrict obfervance of its dictates, may meet others equally defirous of engaging in every plan, which can contribute to extend more widely the knowledge and the practice of the duties of chriftianity. No apprehenfion of invidious fingularity need deter any individual from the hardy enterprife of public reformation. He will in this fociety find himfelf fupported at once by numbers and by refpectability. No defpair of the fuccefs of fo vaft an undertaking fhould difcourage his attempt. He beholds here a moral power, which, if duly exerted, is adequate to every purpofe. Compofed as this Affociation is of the ferious and intelligent of every order, comprifing within it the collective zeal and wifdom of all the active friends of religion, and the influence of the moft exalted ftation, it muft be in

its

its own nature fitted to enforce with the moſt powerful impreſſion the accompliſhment of its moſt extenſive plans. To ſuppoſe it ineffectual, notwithſtanding the ſincere and vigorous exertions of its members, we muſt ſuppoſe that there is in man no tendency to admire and imitate virtue, and in God no diſpoſition to reward and bleſs its efforts ; that there is no morality on earth, and no providence in heaven.

There is another conſideration, my brethren, derived like the former from the peculiar circumſtances of our country, which gives eſpecial importance to our Aſſociation. The fatal progeny of ages of political diſſenſion has been a diſagreement in religious tenets, aggravated into a ferocious bigotry utterly irreconcileable to the mild principles of that revelation which it profeſſes to ſupport. That ſo many centuries of violence ſhould have been terminated by the horrid cataſtrophe of a rebellion perpetrated with the moſt remorſeleſs cruelty, cannot occaſion much ſurpriſe, however it muſt ſhock every humane and pious feeling. But that in this which boaſts to be an age of reaſon, in this age of vaunted philoſophy lofophy and improvement, the fame malignant and unchriftian fpirit fhould again be loofed to its infernal work of maffacre and defolation, and that this too fhould have been done for effectuating the plans of philofophical improvement, which were to give their due energy to all the nobler principles of the human mind; are facts which muft have aftonifhed every impartial man who refpected himfelf as a reafonable being, every chriftian who charitably trufted that the age of bigotry was paft. Probably indeed it had been paft for ever, if no artifices had been employed to ftimulate into activity the latent principles of religious perverfion which ftill lurked in the breaft of ignorance. The uncharitable violence of ancient fuperftition was gradually yielding to the influence of reafon, and the hereditary rancour of political diffenfion was daily foftened by the peaceful habits of focial intercourfe; but thofe who have profeffed " to think for the people," impatient of the regular progrefs of national improvement, and eager to grafp at every inftrument for effecting the accomplifhment of fchemes which fhould at once abolifh every grievance, affociated in the fupport of what they termed an enlightened poli-

cy,

cy, the operation of a principle which reason and religion equally difclaim. In a country thus haraffed at once by ancient and modern divifions, by the half-forgotten bigotry of the days of ignorance revived and excited in the days of philofophy, no more effectual means of working an extenfive moral and religious reformation could be devifed than a voluntary Affociation, comprehending all of every defcription of its people, who are fincerely defirous of invigorating and diffufing the practical influence of chriftianity. Any other fyftem muft experience a more determined oppofition from the prejudices and jealoufies to which it would be expofed. But what ftrong prepoffeffion can be entertained againft thofe, who have no common intereft except that which arifes from a concurrent conviction of the general importance of the object which they purfue, and who invite the co-operation of all without diftinction that are actuated by a fimilar fpirit? You have acted with the liberality of fuch a comprehenfive fyftem. You have folicited the affiftance of the heads of the Romifh church ; and " by what means a friendly intercourfe and co-operation may be beft procured between the clergy of the different perfuafions, ,

persuasions, in promoting those principles and
practices of the christian religion, in which all
sects of christians are agreed," was an inquiry
which early attracted your attention.

And are there not also, my fellow-christians,
circumstances now operating upon our countrymen, which should at this interesting crisis
encourage to its utmost exertions an Association thus singularly adapted to our national situation ?—*When the judgments of the Lord are in
the earth the inhabitants of the world will learn
righteousness.* It is in the days of peace and
prosperity that man forgets his God. He forgets that the blessings which surround him are
the gratuitous bounties of the Almighty ; he
regards them as the creatures of his own pru-
dence and abilities, or at least as independent
of the will of that providence which has long
continued to vouchsafe them. He may from
a compliance with the decent and useful cus-
toms of the world join in external acknow-
ledgments of the sovereignty of the Lord of
heaven and earth ; but his heart, gratified
with the tranquil enjoyment of the good
things of the world, experiences no want, and
acknowledges no dependence—The season of
adversity,

adverfity is the feafon of religious ferioufnefs.
When the gay fcene, which faftened on this
world all the thoughts and wifhes of the profperous, has been diffipated by the ftroke of
misfortune, they can no longer conceal from
their pride their dependant fituation. When
the indulgences of profperity no longer furnifh their gratification to footh the longings of
the human mind, it muft feek in the confola-
tions of religion that hope of lafting happinefs, which the illufions of fublunary pro-
fpects have ceafed to afford. Thus at once
humbled and undeceived, humbled from the
vain notion of his fecurity, and undeceived in
regard to his falfe eftimate of worldly happinefs, man is fitted for liftening with advantage
to the exhortations of thofe who will with
chriftian zeal avail themfelves of the important crifis. Such a crifis is now afforded to you
my brethren. The chaftifement of the Almighty has paffed through our land. His venge-
ance has not indeed been poured out upon us.
We have not drank of the dregs of his dif-
pleafure. But enough of mifery has been
actually inflicted, enough of uncertainty and
apprehenfion has been introduced amongft
thofe who had efcaped the immediate ftroke of
calamity,

calamity, to open unto religious confiderations thofe avenues of the mind, which " the fober fenfuality" of more profperous times had heretofore fhut up—But befides this effect of recalling to religion thofe who had been feduced from it by the habits of the world, I am perfuaded that I fpeak with fufficient authority, when I affert that the public mifery which we have endured, has had in a confiderable degree a falutary influence in awaking the bigoted to an horror of that bigotry, which has difgraced and ftigmatized our country, and to an anxious defire of deriving from the facred oracles themfelves a true conception of the dictates of that religion, which had been fo much perverted and abufed. Oh my brethren, this is not a moment to be loft in inactivity. Renew your exertions. * Call again on the friends of religion to enable you to effect a farther diftribution of the fcriptures. You have done much, but much more remains to be accomplifhed. Adhere to your original propofal, and let the pure light of fcriptural religion fhine into the darkeft corners of your country.

---

* This moft ufeful plan has been fince refumed, and an engagement formed for the diftribution of three thoufand bibles. For this purpofe more than one hundred guineas have been already fubfcribed.

But

But if there fhould be any, and I fear there
are many fuch, whofe minds, inftead of being
foftened into mutual charity by the fenfe of
mutual errors and the fuffering of common
calamity, have been only irritated into a ftill
more rancorous indulgence of that fpirit,
which in the facred name of religion, has
fpread defolation through our country, it is
the duty of an Affociation liberal and enlightened as is that body which I am addreffing,
to labour by every method, by their collective exertions and their private influence, to
mitigate and calm this unchriftian violence,
and to lead their countrymen to a fincere profeffion of the gofpel of him, *who came not to
deftroy mens lives, but to fave them.* The apoftle
tells us, that even *the angels are defirous of looking into* the myftery of human falvation.
What muft be the feelings of one of thofe
fuperior beings, when, in the progrefs of that
gracious difpenfation, in its flow and gradual
operation on the evil tendencies of the human
heart, he beholds the religion of the meek and
benevolent Jefus perverted into a watchword
of violence and outrage ! Strange and mon-
ftrous perverfion ! But let it, as far as is in
your power, be impreffed upon the public

mind

mind that this is not chriftianity, that the
gofpel difowns and reprobates this acrimonious
fpirit, that it is a religion of peace, and forbearance, and brotherly love.

Some account will naturally be expected of
the efforts which the Affociation has made in
the courfe of the laft year for the accomplifhment of its objects : but it muft be remembered that this has been in a peculiar degree a
year of political agitation and apprehenfion of
every kind. The effect of fuch a period is indeed, as I have ftated, favourable to the im-
preffion of ferious exhortation ; but the immediate crifis is unfavourable to the active co-
operation of large numbers, in any extended
fcheme of moral reformation. You have not
however been remifs. You have renewed
your efforts for reftoring the due obfervation
of the fabbath, for eradicating the vice of
perjury, and for reviving the practice of cate-
·chetical inftruction ; you have appropriated a
fum of money to the reduction of the price of
common prayer-books ; and you have particu-
larly directed your attention to the important
bufinefs of national education. With the moft
heart-felt concern indeed do I ftate to this con-
gregation,

gregation, that you have been abfolutely compelled to abandon the execution of that part of
the general fyftem of education, which moft
powerfully recommends itfelf to the charity,
to the policy, and let me add to the juftice of
fociety. The reform of youthful criminals, and
of the unhappy children of convicts, prefented
itfelf to you as an object interefting to every
friend of humanity and religion. The former
without your interference are referved only
for a maturity of profligacy. Already tainted
with vice, rejected by the virtuous part of fociety, encouraged by the intercourfe of the
vicious, and hardened by detection, they live
only to fill up the meafure of their offences,
to furnifh out a melancholy proof of the extreme degree of human depravation. The
latter are in a fituation fcarcely lefs deplorable.
The children of other parents, however ne-
glected, might cafually receive fome faint im-
preffion of moral obligation. They might
fometimes hear the praifes beftowed upon a
virtuous action, and catch with awakened
feelings the fympathy of goodnefs. They
might fometimes witnefs the obfervance of a
religious duty, and be induced to meditate

on

on that great Being who is vifible only to the eye of reafon. But what a growth of abomination muft we look for in the minds of the children of the criminal poor! After every precaution has been employed to guard the heart from the corruptions of human frailty, how powerful is found to be the influence of worldly temptations in withdrawing us from the fervice of our God! What then muft be the moral fituation of a child, who has feen in the example of a parent only a continued leffon of depravity, who has been taught to regard fraud, and violence, and pollution, as the ordinary and neceffary means of fubfiftence, and has learned the exiftence of a Deity only from the blafphemies of execration! Can we abandon thofe novices in the ways of infamy, thofe victims of hereditary vice? Are they to grow up only to be facrificed to the neceffities of public fecurity, to perpetuate the miferable fucceffion of vice and wretchednefs and ignominy? You zealoufly interpofed for their refcue, but you were unequal to the attempt. An Affociation, whofe fund confifts only of the voluntary contributions of its members, was inadequate to the expence of fuch an undertaking. But whilft we recollect that the

wife

wife charity of our fifter-country has inftituted and fupported fuch an afylum for thofe out-
cafts of religion, let us hope that the plan
which you have been compelled to abandon is
not therefore abandoned for ever; let us hope
that it will be efficacioufly adopted by the
public, as indifpenfable to the prefervation of
public morals from the baneful infufion of in-
fant profligacy thus continued from generation to generation, and to the vindication of
public juftice from the cruelty of punifh-
ing with undiftinguifhing feverity what may
almoft be termed involuntary and inevitable
vice—I muft not pafs in filence over a fociety,
which may be faid to have fprung from your
Affociation. " The Howard Society," whofe
object is to relieve the neceffities of the unhappy prifoner, to reform his morals, and to
give employment to his induftry, is a branch
of that parent-ftock of virtue and religion,
which has taken root amongft you, and will
foon I truft overfhadow our now miferable
country.

I have now, my brethren, endeavoured to
fulfil the duty which you had impofed on me,
by ftating the nature and tendency of your
moft

moſt laudable and uſeful inſtitution, the circumſtances which in this country give ſuch an
inſtitution peculiar importance, and the exertions which you have made for the attainment of
your ſalutary purpoſes—Permit me, before I
conclude, to addreſs you with chriſtian ſincerity
in the language of exhortation—You have
aſſociated for the nobleſt purpoſes, and as a
collective body you have done much for their
accompliſhment. But remember, my brethren, that the efficacy of your united mea
ſures depends upon your individual conduct.
—Does then our Aſſociation manifeſt its ſpirit
in the conduct of its own members ? Is it evidently the co-operation of men ſincerely zealous in the advancement of religion, as the
means of promoting at once the preſent and
future happineſs of mankind ? Or is it merely
the temporary expedient of worldly-minded
politicians, ſeeking to reſtrain others by con
ſiderations which have no influence over them
ſelves ? Such a ſcheme muſt be as unſucceſsful, as it would be unworthy—Who will regard your admonitions, if it be not obvious to
the public that yourſelves regard them ? If
your conduct be not diſtinguiſhable from that
of the diſſipated and worldly, what check can
the

the upper claſſes of ſociety receive from your
exhortations ? To them they will appear only
the mockeries of hypocritical grimace. What
effect can they have upon the lower claſſes, if
they behold you practically diſavowing thoſe
precepts which you anxiouſly. recommend
to their obſervance? They will appear only
to be the tricks of human policy, to be one
part of a general ſyſtem of impoſture ? No,
my brethren, to be ſuccefsful you muſt be
ſincere and conſiſtent ; you muſt be penetrated with a ſenſe of the truth and importance of
that religion which you profeſs to ſupport;
and you muſt evince the ſincerity of that conviction by the whole tenor of your conduct—
You will pardon that plainneſs with which I
have addreſſed you. The wide extenſion of
our Aſſociation ſeemed to juſtify the admoni-
tion. Spreading through every rank and order of ſociety, it ſeemed to be in danger of
being aſſimilated to the prevailing manners of
the world, inſtead of diffuſing the corrective
influence of virtue and religion.—Could we
indeed at once adhere to the ſincere and fervid
ſpirit which prompted the formation of this
Aſſociation, and comprehend within it all who
may be deſirous of being enrolled amongſt its
. members,

members, it would afford an unequivocal
fymptom, that, however we may have fuffer-
ed our religious feelings to become languid in
the funfhine of profperity, there is ftill
amongft us a vigorous principle of religious
obligation, which the feafon of trial will
bring into exertion ; it might encourage us to
hope, that, amidft thofe fevere inflictions with
which the divine providence is vifiting the corruptions of the European world, this our
ifland may be permitted to enjoy a comparative tranquillity ; that, whilft in the myfteri-
ous difpenfations of the Almighty the influence of religion feems elfewhere for a time to
give way before the triumphant progrefs of
that infidelity which its qwn corruptions have
engendered, it may here experience a fecure
afylum, until it fhall again be enabled to diffufe itfelf throughout a purified and regene-
rated world ; that this our native land, as it
once before received and cherifhed the learning
and civilization which fled before the brutal
violence of the barbarians of the north, may
again be the chofen fanctuary of the deareft
hopes of mankind chafed by the intellectual
barbarifm of a proud and prefumptuous philofophy.

But

But whatever may be the public confequences of our efforts, whether they fhall in
this great day of vifitation, be effectual in
conciliating the protection of providence, or
only moderate our portion of the general fufferings of a corrupted world, we may reft affured that every fincere and zealous exertion
for the great purpofes of this inftitution fhall
to ourfelves produce its full and adequate effect. The profperity and the fall of empires
are hid in the infcrutable councils of the
Almighty; but as certain as the promifes of
God is the recompenfe of virtue. *The wicked
worketh a deceitful work; but to him that foweth
righteoufnefs, fhall be a fure reward.*

F I N I S.

APPENDIX.

THE fame political caufes which during the laft two years have concurred to impede or reftrain the exertions of the Affociation, have, in the prefent, operated with fimilar, though lefs extended effect, by preventing the attendance, or engroffing the attention of fuch members as from local circumftances were immediately involved in, or connected with the great theatre of action. Thofe however who enjoyed a happy feclufion from, or were lefs deeply interefted in thefe important events, fhould confider themfelves more earneftly called upon by this providential circumftance to devote their time and abilities to the attainment of the great objects of this inftitution. Among thefe one of the moft important has ever been, *the Diffemination of the Holy Scriptures.* The original plan of fubfcription for reducing the price of bibles, fo as to bring the knowledge of the gofpel within the purchafe of the loweft claffes, has been recommenced with ardour, and with a promife of the happieft effects. Already have upwards of one hundred guineas been fubfcribed, and there is the beft founded reafon to believe that the fubfcription will fhortly be fo far extended, that the pious intention of the original inftitution will be carried into full execution.

In purfuance of the outline obferved in the laft Appendix, the next object of their attention was a more *due and exact obfervance of the fabbath ;* and here they again obtained the fanction and concurrence

currence of magiſtracy to enforce a due attention to the exiſting laws on this ſubject. On their application alſo the obſervance of Good-Friday and Chriſtmas day, &c. has been enforced by the chief mágiſtratc of the metropolis. Nor have theſe exertions been altogether fruitleſs, the public ſale of goods, &c. having been in a grcat degree prevented, and even that of ſpirituous liquors couſiderably reſtrained on thoſe days. The attainment of theſe objects muſt however ultimately depend rather on the moral and religious improvement of ſociety, than on the operation of penal ſtatutes.

Independent of the former ſteps taken by the Aſſociation to improve *the Religious Education of Youth*, by a communication with the ſociety of literary teachers, &c. an eſſay on this ſubject has been publiſhed under their auſpices, which has met with the approbation of ſeveral learned and reſpected characters, and under the patronage of ſeveral of the Right Rev. Bench, has been diſtributed in the reſpective dioceſes of this kingdom, accompanied with an Addreſs, and Queries from the Aſſociation, for the purpoſe of obtaining more general and correct information on the ſubject. Theſe meaſures are preparatory to a communication with government for the adoption of a more enlarged and enlightened ſyſtem of education for the lower claſſes of ſociety. The Aſſociation have at the ſame time continued to recommend, and to afford their accuſtomed encouragement to the extenſion of catechetical lectures, and they are happy to find that the benefits of this excellent mode of inſtruction are becoming more widely diffuſed and more ſenſibly felt.

Among the various plans undertaken or encouraged by the Aſſociation, it could not be expected that ſimilar ſucceſs ſhould attend upon each, and they are concerned to ſtate, that from a concurrence of cauſes and events, the eſtabliſhment for the

Reform

Reform of the Criminal Poor has failed to produce the beneficial effects fo rationally and ardently expected on its firft inftitution. The attempt however has not been totally unproductive of good, and there is reafon to hope, that at a period of more confirmed tranquillity this object will engage the attention of government ; as the practicability and advantages of the inftitution, on a more enlarged fcale, and with more comprehenfive powers, have been evidently demonftrated. In another line the exertions of the Affociation in favour of the lower claffes of fociety have been attended with happier fuccefs ; *the plan for the encouragement of fervants*, is now nearly matured, is patronifed by characters of the firft rank and ftation, and bids fair to be carried into the fulleft effect. Nor can there be a doubt, but it would be productive of the moft beneficial confequences, not only to thofe who would derive immediate benefit from the inftitution, but to fociety in general, whofe well-being and happinefs is intimately connected with and dependant on the good or ill conduct of this clafs of perfons. Emanating from the Affociation, and compofed principally of its members, though now forming a feparate inftitution, *the Howard Society* next claims our attention. The objects and views of this eftablifhment, and the progrefs made towards their attainment, have already been explained to the public, in the original addrefs and the quarterly report of this fociety. It may not, however, be improper to obferve, that the improved condition of the *Four Courts Marfhalfea*, and *Bridewell*, the two prifons vifited, and the happy change produced in the manners and conduct of the inhabitants, afford the ftrongeft proof of the fuccefs of their exertions, and form the beft eulogium on the labours of the fociety.

Though little apparent effect has been produced by the efforts of the Affociation, to ftem the rage

for

for lottery infurance, which fo univerfally infects the lower claffes of fociety, yet have they continued to publifh cautionary tracts and tales on this fubject, in the hope that they may imperceptibly open the eyes of the deluded multitude, and convince them of the abfurdity, as well as criminality, of thus engaging in a conteft of ignorance and weaknefs againft fraud and knowledge, where the hazard of lofs is reduced to almoft a certainty, where fuccefs could not produce happinefs, but defeat muft be attended with certain ruin.

With a view to the moral and religious inftruction of the lower claffes of fociety, the Affociation have continued to diftribute a variety of tracts on this fubject; among thefe, as one of the moft important, they have encouraged the re-publication of The Whole Duty of Man, in a fmaller fize, and at a cheaper rate, than the prefent edition, to bring it within the purchafe of almoft the loweft clafs of fociety. A confiderable and refpectable lift of fubfcribers have already patronized the work, and it will fhortly be publifhed.

From this detail it will be evident, that though fomething has been done, much yet remains to be performed, in the arduous tafk of difcountenancing Vice, and promoting the Caufe of Religion and Virtue. To this tafk the Affociation wifh to call the attention, and to folicit the co-operation of all their members; and in doing fo, they, with little variation, adopt an addrefs lately prefented to them by one of their moft refpected members, in the following words.

" A Member of the Affociation, who has its interefts warmly at heart, who views with pleafure your laudable efforts to fupprefs Vice and promote Religion and Virue, and the happy effects they have already produced, indulges the fond hope, that you will

will perfevere in your exertions, and not fuffer that zeal, which has hitherto animated you, to fink into defpondency, or die away in languor and luke-warmnefs."

" Your deliberations have been interrupted by the unhappy difturbances of the country for many months paft; but as it may be hoped tranquillity is now returning, your zeal and activity will revive with it. If you are perfuaded, that difcountenancing Vice, and promoting the Practice of Religion and Virtue, are the fureft means under heaven of preventing the recurrence of the calamities which this country has experienced, you will not fuffer your ardour to abate, but will, with redoubled vigour, meet the torrent of vice and infidelity which had well nigh overwhelmed your country, and ftill threatens fur-ther devaftation upon it. Will any defponding mem-ber fay, We have laboured for above fix years, and our labour has been in vain? To fuch member I would anfwer, you cannot know that your labour has been in vain; bad as things have been, they might have been much worfe; and there is every reafon to believe, that had an inftitution, fuch as yours, been eftablifhed in this country at an earlier period, it would have tended much either to pre-vent or to alleviate the horrors of the late rebellion. Had every cabbin been furnifhed with a bible, had the bleffings of education been extended to the cot-tages of the poor, would not their minds have been enlightened, their manners foftened, and that fero-city of temper (which has imprinted an indelible ftain on the national character) been melted down into a mild, gentle, and Chriftian difpofition?—If fuch be the cafe, fhall we not perfevere in our labour of love? Shall we not exert our moft ftrenuous efforts to bring about fo defirable a change? Much is ex-pected of us. A refpectable fociety, inftituted fome years before ours, has merged in ours; and the public

lic have a claim upon us for the good which that
fociety would have produced, and alfo for what we
have pledged ourfelves to perform ?—Should we now
grow languid and defponding, how fatal would the
confequence be ? (to ufe the words of that excellent
member who preached our firft fermon) " How foon
" would public derifion and contempt crufh our puny
" and abortive efforts ? And how would the prece-
" dent of our ill fuccefs check every future attempt
" to reform or inftruct a licentious and irreligious
" age ?"

Let us then, from this moment, devote ourfelves
heartily to the great work we have undertaken; let
us not be weary in well-doing. Our caufe is a good
one; and we have reafon to hope that Providence
will crown our labours with fuccefs, and confer upon
us, at the laft day, the reward of thofe " who turn
many to righteoufnefs," provided we perfevere unto
the end with conftancy and refolution.

Receipts and Payments of the Affociation for difcountenancing Vice and promoting the Practice of Religion and Virtue, from 1ft June, 1798, (when the laft Account was publifhed) to 1ft July, 1799.

RECEIPTS.

	£.	s.	d.
Balance in favour of the Affociation, 1ft June, 1798 - - -	74	0	7½
Subfcriptions - - -	208	3	3
Donation from his Grace the Lord Primate	22	15	0
Do. from Perfons not Members -	9	2	0
Tracts and pamphlets fold - -	9	3	7
	£.323	4	5½

PAYMENTS.

	£.	s.	d.
Printing the following tracts, &c. faleable at reduced prices, or diftributed gratis			
1000 Sermon, preached before the Affociation, 22d May, 1798, by the Right Rev. T. L. O'Beirne, Lord Bifhop of Offory - - -		. .	
3000 Exhortation to the duty of catechifing - -			
1000 Expoftulations to the higher claffes	81	17	10
500 Effay on manners and education			
1000 Reflections on Chriftmas			
1000 Prayers for infirmaries			
250 Plan for encouragement of fervants			
500 Refolutions for obfervance of the Sabbath, fecond edition -			
1500 Abftract of the laws in force, for better obfervation of the Sabbath			
Premiums and other expences incurred by catechetical examinations in 1799	14	3	0
Advertifing - - -	13	3	9½
Printing and Stationary - -	24	15	2½
Affiftant Secretary and Meffenger -	72	17	4½
Incidental and petty charges -	1	12	4½
Balance in favour of the Affociation, 1ft July, 1799. -	114	14	10½
£.	323	4	5½

E

L I S T

MEMBERS OF THE ASSOCIATION.

Thus marked *, are Subfcribers to the Fund.

His Excellency CHARLES, Marquis CORNWALLIS, Lord Lieutenant General and General Governor of Ireland, Prefident.

A
* His Grace the Lord Archbifhop of Armagh
* Right Hon. Lord Arden
* Earl of Altamont
Captain Chriftopher Abbott
* John Allen, Efq.
* Thomas Acton, Efq.
* Rev. Dr. Alcock
* Rev. George Alcock
* Lt. Col. William Alexander
* Rev. John Alexander
* Rev. Dr. Allott, Dean of Raphoe
* Rt. Hon. Thomas Andrews, Lord Mayor
* Rev. Henry Annefley
* Hon. and Rev. William Annefley, Dean of Down
James Arbuckle, Efq.
Rev. Frederick Arbuthnot
Rev. Alex. Arbuthnot
* Rev. Wm. Jones Armftrong
* Rev. Wm. Armftrong
* Rev. Jonathan Afh
* Rev. Ifaac Afh
* Rev. Nicholas Afh
* Rev. Wm. Athill
* Jackfon Wray Atkinfon, Efq.
* Rev. Gilbert Auften

B
Rt. Hon. Earl of Belvedere
* Rev. Walter Bagot
* Chriftopher Bagot, Efq.
* Rev. Chas. Emilius Bagot
Counfellor Ball
* Rev. John Ball
* Rev. John Barker
Rev. Thomas Barry
* Rev. Philip Barry
* Rev. Edward Barton, Archdeacon of Ferns
* Rev. Leflie Batterfby
Rev. Henry Bayly
* Rev. P. Bayly
* Rev. Edward Bayly
* Rev. Edward Beattie
* Rev. Dr. Beaufort
* Rev. Dr. Benning
* M. G. Bettefworth
* John Berry, Efq.
* John Claud. Beresford, Efq.
* Rev. Charles Cobbe Beresford
* Rev. George Beresford, Dean of Kilmore
* Rev. Edward Berwick, Vicar of Leixlip
* Rev. Dr. Blundell, Dean of Kildare

Rev.

* Rev. William Blundell
* Richard Bolton, Efq.
* Richard Paul Bonham, Efq.
* Rev. Richard Bourne
* Hon. and Rev. Rich. Bourke
Rev. Henry Boyd
Maj. Gen. Wm. Brady.
* John Brett, Efq.
* Rev. David Brickell
* Rev. John Brinkley
Rev. William Briftow
William Brooke, Efq.
Rev. Richard Brooke
Rev. Wm. Brooke, Vicar of Granard
Arthur Browne, Efq. LL. D. S. F. T. C. D.
* Rev. Chaworth Browne
* Rev. Thomas Brownrigg
* Dr. Bryanton
* Rev. Dr. Burrowes
Rev. Kildare Burrowes
Rev. Edmund Burton, Archdeacon of Tuam
Charles Kendal Bufhe, Efq.
* Rev. Richard Butler
* Rev. Chriftopher Butfon, Dean of Waterford

C.
* His Grace the Lord Archbifhop of Cafhel
* Right Hon. Earl of Charlemont
* Earl Camden
* Right Rev. Lord Bifhop of Clogher
* Right Rev. Lord Bifhop of Clonfert
* Right Rev. and Hon. Lord Bifhop of Cork
* Right Rev. Lord Bifhop of Cloyne
* Turner Camac, Efq.
* Rev. Robert Cane
* Alderman Carleton
* Rev. Peter Carleton, Dean of Killaloe

Alexander Carroll, Efq.
* Captain John Cafh
* Richard Cave, Efq.
* Rev. C. B. Caulfield, Archdeacon of Clogher
* Rev. Charles Caulfield
* Rt. Hon. Sir Henry Cavendifh, Bart.
* John Chambers, Efq.
* George Chinnery, Efq.
Rev. Dr. Cleaver
James Cleghorn, Efq. M. D.
* Hon. and Rev. Wm. Montgomery Cole
* Rev. Charles Coleman
* Mathew Coleman, Efq.
Richard Collis, Efq.
* William Cooke, Efq.
Captain William Cope
* Right Hon. Ifaac Corry
* Rev. Thomas Conolly Cowan
* Rev. Jacob Cramer
* Rev. Dr. M. Cramer
Rev. George Crane
* Rev. Henry Crofton, Foundling Hofpital
* Rev. Henry Crofton, Royal Hofpital
* Morgan Crofton, Efq.
* Morgan Crofton, jun. Efq.
Edward Croker, Efq.
* Rev. John Cromie
* Hon. Juftice Crookfhank
George Crookfhank, Efq.
* Edward Crofbie, Efq.
* John Crofthwaite, Efq.
Charles Coftello, Efq.
* Delacherois Crommelin, Efq.
* George Cullen, Efq.
* William Cuthbert, Efq.

D.
* His Grace the Archbifhop of Dublin
* Right Rev. Lord Bifhop of Dromore
John Dawfon, Efq.

Rev.

* Rev. Richard Dawſon
* Hon Juſtice Day
* John Deane, Eſq.
* Joſeph Deane, Eſq.
* Rev. Richard Deſpard
* Steph. Dickſon, Eſq. M. D.
* Rev. Wm. Digby, Dean of Clonfert
* William Diſney, Eſq.
* Rev. Robert Diſney
* Rev. Brabazon Diſney
* Thomas Diſney, Eſq.
* Rev. Dr. Dobbin
* Francis Dobbs, Eſq.
* Captain Jeremiah D'Olier
* Rev. Samuel Downing
* Rev. Dr. Drought
* Rev. Richard Drury
Hon. Charles Dundas
* Rev. James Dunn

E

* Right Rev. Lord Biſhop of Elphin
John Eccles, Bſq.
* Iſaac Ambroſe Eccles, Eſq.
Rev. John Elgee
* Rev. Dr. Thomas Elliſon
Rev. Dr. Thomas Elrington, F.T.C.D.
* Gaſper Erke, Eſq.
* Rev. Joſiah Erſkine
* Counſellor Eſpinaſſe
* George Evans, Eſq.
* Rev. Mr. Evans
Thomas Everard, Eſq.

F

* Earl Fitzwilliam
* Counteſs Fitzwilliam
* Right Rev. Lord Biſhop of Ferns
* Frederick Falkiner, Eſq.
Rev. Wm. Lynar Fawcett
Rev. Joſeph Faviere
* Rev. John Fea
* Mr. John Ferrar
Rev. Dr. Robert Poole Finch
Rev. Quintin Finlay

* Rev. Joſeph Fitzpatrick
Rev. Stephen Fletcher
Right Hon. Wm. Forward
* Mr. George Forſter
* Rev. Nicholas Forſter
* Right Hon. John Foſter, Speaker of the Houſe of Commons
* Rev. Robert Fowler, Archdeacon of Dublin
* John Fox, Eſq.
* David Freeman, Eſq.
* Rev. David Freeman
* Counſellor Robert French
* Richard Frizell, ſen. Eſq.

G

* Rev. Thomas Gamble
* Rev. Samuel Gerard
* James Gibbons, Eſq.
* Rev. William Gimingham
* John Godley, Eſq.
* Joſeph Goff, Eſq.
* Rev. Thomas Goff
Rev. Mr. Gorman
* Rev. John Grant
* Rev. Richard Graves, D. D. F. T. C. D.
* Rev. Thomas Grace
* Rev. Thomas Graves, Dean of Ardfert
* Rev. George Graydon
* Robert Graydon, Eſq.
* Rev. Richard Grier
* Rev. Geo. Leſlie Greſſon
* Richard Griffith, Eſq.
* Rev. Charles Grove
* Rev. Dr. Grueber
* Rev. Dr. Hoſea Guinneſs
* Rev. Wm. Gwynne

H

Rev. Dr. Hales
Rev. Dr. Hall, S. F. T. C. D.
William Hall, Eſq.
* Rev. Alexander Hamilton
Rev. Dr. James Archibald Hamilton
* John Hamilton, Eſq.

Rev.

* Rev. Hans Hamilton
* Alexander Hamilton, Efq.
Edward Harman, Efq.
* Rev. Singleton Harpur
* Rev. John Ifaac Harrifon
Rev. John Harvey
* Rev. James Haftings, Arch-
deacon of Glandelagh
Rev. Dr. Chriftopher Harvey
Rev. John Haughton
* Hugh Henry, Efq.
* Rev. Edward Herbert
Rev. Arthur Herbert
* Henry Hewitt, Efq.
Hon. and Rev. John Hewitt,
Dean of Cloyne
* Rev. Ambrofe Hickey
* Edward Hill, Efq.
Dr. Edward Hill
* Rev. Averill Hill
* Rev. T. D. Hincks
* Lewis Hqdgfon, Efq.
Peter Holmes, Efq.
* Robert Holmes, Efq.
Rev. Philip Homan
Sir Francis Hopkins, Bart.
* Francis Hopkins, Efq. M. D.
* John Hopkins, Efq.
* Hugh Howard, Efq.
* Rohert Howard, Efq.
* Rev. Dr. Hume, Dean of
Derry
Hon. and Rev. Abraham Hely
Hutchinfon
* Sir Francis Hutchinfon, Bt.
* Rev. James Hutchinfon,
Archdeacon of Achonry
Rev. Francis Hutchefon

J

* Alexander Jaffray, Efq.
* Alexander Jaffray, jun. Efq.
Alderman William James
* Captain Meredith Jenkin
Rev. John Jephfon
Rev. William Jephfon

* Edmund Johnfton, Efq.
* Rev. Thomas Jones
* Rev. Wm. Dunkin Jones
Rev. Crinus Irwin
John Irwin, Efq.
* Rev. James Irwin
K·
* Right Hon. Earl of King-
fton
* Right Hon. Lord Bifhop of
Kildare
* Right Rev. Rord Bifhop of
Killalla
Right Rev. Lord Bifhop of
Killaloe
* Right Rev. and Hon. Lord
Bifhop of Kilmore
Right Hon. Lord Kilmaine
* Right Hon. Ld. Kilwarden
Rev. John Kearney, D. D.,
Provoft of Trinity College
* Rev. Dr. Michael Kearney
Rev. John Keating
* Rev. John Kellet
* Rev. John Kennedy
* Rev. Nicholas Ward Ken-
nedy
* Rev. Dr. Kennedy, Vicar of
Kilmore
Rev. John Kenny, Vicar Ge-
neral of Cork
Rev. Robert Kenny
* Thomas King, Efq.
* Rev. Thomas Kingfbury
* Chas. Berkeley Kippax, Efq.
* Alexander Kirkpatrick, Efq.
Rev. Walter Blake Kirwan
* Alex. Knox, Efq.
L
His Grace the Duke of Lein-
fter
Rt. Hon. Lord Longueville
* John Ladaveze, Efq.
Rev. George Lambert
* Rev. Dr. Lamilliere
* Rev.

* Rev. Archdeacon Lamilliere
Major William Lane
* Rev. Ed. Francis Lascelles
* Right Hon. David Latouche
* John Latouche, Esq.
* Peter Latouche, Esq.
* David Latouche, jun. Esq.
* Charles Laurent, Esq.
* Rev. John Leahy
* Rev. Edward Ledwich
- Rev. William Ledwich
Rev. Giles Lee
* John Leigh, Esq.
* Rev. John Letablere
* Rev. John Lewis
* Rev. Dr. Little
* Edward Litton, Esq.
* Rev. Verney Lovett
* Rev. Dr. Wm. Lodge
Rev. George Lowe
* Gorges Lowther, Esq.
Henry Lyons, Esq.
* Rev. Dr. Thomas Lyster
* Rev. John Lyster
M
* Earl of Meath
* Right Hon. Lord Bishop of
    Meath
* Rev. Robert M'Askie
* Rev. Dr. M'Dowell
Rev. Henry M'Clean
Rev. William M'Laughlin
* John Macauley, Esq.
* Rev. Wm. Magee, F.T.C.D.
* Rev. Daniel M'Neil
* Rev. Thomas M'Mahon
Alderman Richard Manders
* Rev. Edward Mangin
* Mr. Wm. Martley
* Peter Maturin, Esq.
* Wm. Maturin, Esq. Secre-
    tary.
Rev. Henry Maturin
Rev. Wm. Mauleverer
* Rev. Henry Maxwell
* Rev. James Maxwell, Sec.
* Rev. Dr. Wm. Maxwell

* John Waring Maxwell, Esq.
* Robert Mayne, Esq.
* Rev. Richard Meade
Hon. Baron Metge
* Rev. George Miller, D. D.
    F. T. C. D.
* Rev. Oliver Miller
* Rev. John Miller
* Humphry Minchin, Esq.
* Rev. James Montgomery
Rev. Alexander Montgomery
* Rev. Robert Montgomery
Rev. Mr. Moor
* Captain Moor.
* Rev. Hugh Moore
* Mrs. Hannah More, Bristol.
* Rev. Allen Morgan
* Rev. James Morgan
Rev. Charles Mosse
Rev. Hector Munro
Rev. Henry Murray
* Rev. Doctor Samuel Murray.
N.
* Thomas Needham, Esq.
* Rev. Robert Nixon
* Thomas Newenham, Esq.
Sir Edw. Newenham, Knt.
* Wm. Worth. Newenham,
    Esq.
* Wm. T. Newenham, Esq.
Robert O'Callaghan Newen-
    ham, Esq.
* Edward Worth Newenham,
    Esq.
Major Nicolls
* Rev. Brinsley Nixon
* Rev. Robert Nixon
Brabazon Noble, Esq.
O
* Lord Visc. Oxmantown
* Right Rev. Lord Bishop of
    Ossory
* Rev. Dr. O'Connor
* Wm. Meade Ogle, Esq.
* Charles O'Hara, Esq.
* Rev. Hugh O'Neil
Thomas Ormsby, Esq.

Rev.

Rev. Dr. Owen, North Wales

P

Rev. Henry Palmer, Archdeacon of Offory.
* Roger Palmer, Efq.
Rev. Henry Pafley
Rev. Thos. Chriftmas Paul
* Rt. Hon. Thomas Pelham
* Rev. Philip Perceval.
* Robert Perceval, Efq. M. D.
John Pollock, Efq.
* Jofeph Pollock, Efq.
* Hon. and Rev. John Pomeroy.
* Rev. Richard Powell
Robert Powell, Efq.
William Prefton, Efq.
Rev. Edward Price
* Rev. Mr. Prince, of London.
* Major General Pringle
Rev. Thos. Prior, F. T. C. D.

R

* Rev. John Radcliffe
* Counfellor Redford
Rev. Hugh Reynolds
* Rev. Edward Richardfon
* Jonathan Bruce Roberts, Efq.
Rev. Peter Roberts,
John Roberts, Efq.
* Rev. Thomas Robinfon
* Guftavus Rochfort, Efq.
Rev. George Rogers
* Sam. Rofborough, Efq,
Rev. John Rofe
Thomas Rothwell, Efq.
John Rothwell, Efq.
* Clotworthy Rowley, Efq.
William Rowley, Efq.
* Rev. Robert Ruffell
* Rev. Dudley Chas. Ryder

S

Rt. Hon. and Rev. Lord Vifcount Strangford
* George Sandford, Efq.
Rev. Chriftopher Savage
* Art. Saunders, Efq. M. D.
* Morley Saunders, Efq.

* Rev. James Sautin
* John Schoales, Efq.
* George Schoales, Efq.
* George Schoales, Efq. of London
* Thos. Purdon Scott
* Rev. Dr. George Sealy
Rev. Archdeacon Seaton
Rev. George Shaw, of London
Rev. Wentworth Shield
* Rev. Walter Shirley
Rev. Dr. Simcocks
* Hugh Skeys, Efq.
* John Skeys, Etq.
* Rev. Mathew Sleater
Mr. Wm. Sleater
* Ralph Smyth, Efq.
Hon. Baron Smith
William Smith, Efq.
* Rev. Dr. Thomas Smith
* Rev. George Smith
* Rev. William Spence
* Rev. Dr. Stack
* Wm. Stamer, Efq.
Daniel Steuart, Efq.
* Rev. Hugh Stewart
* Rev. Henry Stewart
* John Stewart, Efq.
* Hon. Robert Stewart
Charles Stewart, Efq.
* Henry Stewart, Efq.
* Rev. Dr. Stokes
* Rev. Gabriel Stokes
* Whitley Stokes, Efq. M. D. F. T. C. D.
* Rev. James Stopford
* Rev. Jofeph Stopford, Charleville
* Rev. Jofeph Stopford, F. T. C. D.
Rev. Wm. Stopford
* Lieut. General Straton
* Rev. James Stubbs
* Rev. Thomas Sutton
* Rev. Samuel Synge, Archdeacon of Killaloe
* Sir Walter Synott, Bart.

His

T

His Grace the Lord Archbi-
ſhop of Tuam.
Hon. and Rev. Edward Tay-
lor
* Rev. William Tew
* John Tew, Eſq.
* Rev. Thomas Thompſon,
Dean of Killalla.
Richard Thwaites, Eſq.   .
* Rev. Thomas Tighe   ·
* Francis Tipping, Eſq.   ›
Rt. Hon. John Toler, Attor-
ney General
Dr. Townſend
* Rev. Power Trench
Frederick Trench, Eſq.
* Rev. Thos. Trench
* Thos. Stocker Triphook,
Eſq.
* Rev. Dr. Robert Truel
* Rev. Peter Turpin

V

* William Vavaſour, Eſq.
* Rev. James Verſchoyle,
Dean of St. Patrick
* Rev. Robert Vicars
Rev. Richard Vincent
* Rev. Hemſworth Uſher
* Rev. John Uſher, F. T.
C. D.
Rev. Henry Cornelius Uſher,
F. T. C. D.

W

* Rev. John Waddy
Robert Watſon Wade, Eſq.
*, Rev. Wm. Wakeley
* Rev. Chamberlen Walker
* Rev. John Walker, F. T.
C. D.

Wm. Walker, Eſq. Recorder
* Rev. John Walſh
* Rev. Raphael Walſh, Dean
of Dromore
* Rev. C. M. Warburton,
Dean of Ardagh
* Bernard Ward, Eſq.
* Mr. Wm. Watſon
* Mr. Wm. Watſon, jun.
.Treaſurer
Rev. John Webb
* Commiſ. Chriſtmas Weekes
* Mathew Weld, Eſq.
* Rev. Arthur Weldon
* Rev. Anthony Weldon
* Luke White, Eſq.
* Rev. Wm. White
* Rev. James Whitelaw
Geo. Boleyn Whitney, Eſq.
* Rev. Irwin Whitty
* Abraham Wilkinſon, Eſq.
* Rev. John Williamſon
* Rev. Andrew Wilſon
Rev. Joſeph Wilſon
* Benjamin Woodward, Eſq.
* Rev. Richard Woodward
Henry Woodward, Eſq.
* Ben. Blake Woodward, Eſq.
* Rev. Henry Woodward
* Sir Wm. Worthington, Knt.
* Wm. Henry Worthington,
Eſq. Charnas, Stafford
* Rev. Guſtavus Wybrants
Stephen Wybrants, Eſq.
* Rev. Henry Wynne
* Rev. Richard Wynne
* Robert Wynne, Eſq.
* Wiliiam Wynne, Eſq.

Y

* Rt. Hon. Lord Yelverton.

9783337002619

*9 7 8 3 3 3 7 0 0 2 6 1 9 *